SO, YOU'RE SAYING THERE'S A CHANCE?

RANDOM FACTS, FIGURES & ODDS

Published by Willow Creek Press, Inc.
P.O. Box 147, Minocqua, Wisconsin 54548

Printed in the United States

SO, YOU'RE SAYING THERE'S A CHANCE?

RANDOM FACTS, FIGURES & ODDS

WILLOW CREEK PRESS®

25%
OF AMERICAN MEN ARE NOW SIX FEET OR TALLER COMPARED TO ONLY 4% IN 1900.

- -

ODDS AN ADULT BELIEVES IN BIGFOOT.
1 IN 6

A NEW BABY USUALLY
DEPRIVES EACH OF IT'S
PARENTS AROUND
350-400
HOURS OF SLEEP IN
THE FIRST YEAR.

- - - - - - - - - - - - - - - - - - - -

OVER 96%
OF AMERICAN HOUSEHOLDS
PURCHASE BANANAS AT
LEAST ONCE A MONTH.

- - - - - - - - - - - - - - - - - - - -

ODDS OF BEING
KILLED BY LIGHTNING.
1 IN 2,320,000

ODDS OF GETTING
THE FLU THIS YEAR.
1 IN 10

- -

60%
OF THE COUNTRY OF
LIECHTENSTEIN'S GDP IS
GENERATED FROM THE
SALE OF FALSE TEETH.

- -

ODDS THAT A U.S. CITIZEN
WILL BECOME A MILLIONAIRE.
1 IN 30

HICCUPS USUALLY LAST FOR
5 MINUTES.

- -

ODDS AN AMERICAN HAS AT LEAST ONE TATTOO.
1 IN 4.8

- -

63%
OF PET OWNERS SLEEP WITH THEIR PETS.

WHEN WATER FREEZES
IT EXPANDS BY

9%.

ODDS THAT AN ADULT MALE
IS AFRAID OF SPIDERS.

1 IN 37

30%

OF PEOPLE REFUSE TO
SIT ON PUBLIC TOILET SEATS.

ODDS OF DYING IN AN ON-THE-JOB ACCIDENT.

1 IN 48,000

- -

1 IN 4

PEOPLE ADMIT TO SEARCHING IN THEIR HOST'S MEDICINE CABINETS.

WOMEN MAKE UP

49%

OF THE WORLDS
POPULATION.

- -

ODDS OF BEING
BORN A TWIN IN
NORTH AMERICA.

1 IN 90

ABOUT

5%

OF PEOPLE DREAM IN COLOR.

- -

ODDS OF BEING
THE VICTIM OF A
SERIOUS CRIME IN
YOUR LIFETIME.

1 IN 20

- -

22%

OF PEOPLE SKIP LUNCH DAILY.

85%
OF WOMEN WEAR THE WRONG BRA SIZE.

ODDS OF PICKING ALL "SWEET SIXTEEN" TEAMS IN THE NCAA BASKETBALL BRACKET.
1 IN 1,900,000

MORE THAN
10%
OF THE WORLD'S SALT IS USED TO DE-ICE AMERICAN ROADS.

90%
OF PEOPLE DEPEND ON ALARM CLOCKS TO WAKE UP.

- -

ODDS OF BEING STRUCK BY LIGHTNING.
1 IN 576,000

- -

21%
OF PEOPLE DON'T MAKE THEIR BED IN THE MORNING.

ODDS OF AN AMERICAN HAVING
AT LEAST ONE CONTAINER OF
ICE CREAM IN THE FREEZER.

9 IN 10

EVERY POSSIBLE

3 CHARACTER

.COM DOMAIN HAS BEEN
REGISTERED.

MEN ARE

25%

MORE LIKELY THAN WOMEN
TO RUN STOP LIGHTS.

YOU TAKE OVER

23,000

BREATHS EVERY DAY.

- -

95%

OF THE CREATURES ON EARTH ARE
SMALLER THAN A CHICKEN EGG.

- -

ABOUT

8%

OF THE STUDENTS AT
THE DUNKIN' DONUTS
TRAINING CENTER FAIL
THE SIX-WEEK COURSE.

19%
OF MEN SAY THEY WOULDN'T MIND BEING STUPID AS LONG AS THEY HAD THE PERFECT BODY.

- -

ODDS AN ADULT SHOWERS LESS THAN ONCE A WEEK.
1 IN 100

ODDS OF BEING HIT BY A METEOR.
1 IN 182,138,880,000,000

- -

THE EARTH IS TURNING TO DESERT AT A RATE OF
40
SQUARE MILES PER DAY.

- -

ODDS OF A PERSON IN THE MILITARY WINNING THE MEDAL OF HONOR.
1 IN 11,000

37%
OF PEOPLE HAVE NEVER MOVED FROM THEIR HOMETOWN.

- -

THE EARTH EXPERIENCES OVER
50,000
EARTHQUAKES A YEAR.

- -

A JELLYFISH IS
95%
WATER.

ODDS THAT A DEATH CERTIFICATE IS INCORRECT.

1 IN 3

64%

OF AMERICANS OWN A SMARTPHONE. 67% CHECK IT EVEN IF IT DIDN'T RING.

THE HUMAN BODY CONTAINS
59,650
MILES OF BLOOD VESSELS.

- -

ODDS A MAN HAS
CRIED AT A WEDDING.
1 IN 11

- -

ODDS AN ADULT EATS A
BAGEL FOR BREAKFAST.
1 IN 25

THE AVERAGE AMERICAN USES

730

CRAYONS BY THE AGE OF 10.

- - - - - - - - - - - - - - - - - -

ODDS YOUR NEW YEAR'S
RESOLUTION WAS TO
LOSE WEIGHT.

1 IN 5

- - - - - - - - - - - - - - - - - -

THE AVERAGE
PORCUPINE HAS

30,000

SPIKES.

YOUR BRAIN USES

25%

OF ALL THE OXYGEN
YOU BREATHE.

- - - - - - - - - - - - - - - - - - - -

ODDS OF SURVIVING
A PLANE CRASH.

1 IN 2.6

- - - - - - - - - - - - - - - - - - - -

OXYGEN, CARBON, HYDROGEN
AND NITROGEN MAKE UP

90%

OF THE HUMAN BODY.

ODDS OF SPOTTING A UFO TODAY.

1 IN 3,000,000

- -

71%

OF AMERICANS NAMED ALEXANDER HAMILTON AS A U.S. PRESIDENT EVEN THOUGH HE WAS NOT.

ODDS OF CORRECTLY CALLING A COIN FLIP 27 TIMES IN A ROW.

1 IN 134,000,000

- -

ODDS AN ADULT'S FAVORITE SPORT IS GOLF.

1 IN 25

THERE IS
200 TIMES
MORE GOLD IN THE WORLD'S
OCEANS THAN HAS BEEN MINED.

- -

THE WORLD'S
8 RICHEST
MEN HAVE AS MUCH
MONEY AS THE POOREST
HALF, 3.6 BILLION PEOPLE.

- -

ODDS OF BECOMING
A PRO ATHLETE.
1 IN 22,000

A 1 MINUTE KISS BURNS

26

CALORIES.

- - - - - - - - - - - - - - - -

AVERAGE LIFE SPAN OF A MODERN TOILET IS

50 YEARS.

- - - - - - - - - - - - - - - -

THE WORLD HAS BEEN AT PEACE ONLY

8%

OF THE TIME OVER THE LAST 3,500 YEARS.

AMERICANS EAT
35,000
TONS OF PASTA A YEAR.

ODDS THAT A CHILD
SLEEPWALKS.
1 IN 10

ODDS OF FINDING A
FOUR-LEAF CLOVER
ON YOUR FIRST TRY.
1 IN 10,000

ODDS OF BOWLING A
PERFECT 300 GAME.
1 IN 11,500

72%
OF PEOPLE EAVESDROP.

ODDS OF AN AMERICAN
SPEAKING CHEROKEE.
1 IN 15,000

ODDS OF CHOOSING A PERFECT NCAA BASKETBALL BRACKET.

1 IN 9,223,372,036,854,775,808

- - - - - - - - - - - - - - - - - - - -

53%
OF WOMEN DON'T LEAVE HOME WITHOUT MAKEUP ON.

- - - - - - - - - - - - - - - - - - - -

ODDS OF WINNING IF YOU CHALLENGE A TRAFFIC TICKET IN COURT.

1 IN 3

ODDS OF YOUR CHILD BEING A GENIUS.
1 IN 250

ODDS OF STRIKING IT RICH ON *ANTIQUES ROADSHOW.*
1 IN 60,000

ODDS A TAX FILER WILL REQUEST AN EXTENSION.
1 IN 12

45%

OF AMERICANS DON'T KNOW THAT THE SUN IS A STAR.

- -

ODDS OF BEING AUDITED BY THE IRS.

1 IN 160

- -

YOU BEGIN TO FEEL THIRSTY WHEN YOUR BODY LOSSES

1%

OF WATER.

YOU BLINK
10,000,000
TIMES EVERY YEAR.

- -

96%
OF CANDLES SOLD ARE
PURCHASED BY WOMEN.

THE HUMAN HEART CREATES
ENOUGH PRESSURE TO SQUIRT
30 FEET
OF BLOOD.

- -

THE INTERNET HAS
4,200,000,000
USERS.

- -

ODDS THAT A CATASTROPHIC
ASTEROID WILL COLLIDE
WITH EARTH IN THE
NEXT 100 YEARS.
1 IN 5,000

1 IN 3

DOG OWNERS SAY THEY HAVE TALKED TO THEIR PETS ON THE PHONE.

IT TAKES

1 WEEK

TO MAKE A JELLY BEAN.

60%

OF ALL ATHEISTS AND AGNOSTICS SAY THEY OWN AT LEAST ONE BIBLE.

THE AVERAGE PERSON SPENDS 2 YEARS ON THE PHONE IN THEIR LIFETIME.

- -

BRAZIL COVERS 50% OF THE SOUTH AMERICAN CONTINENT.

32%
OF SINGLES POLLED THINK
THEY WILL MEET THEIR
FUTURE MATE ONLINE.

THE VATICAN HAS

5 POPES

PER SQUARE MILE.

85%
OF OBSCENE CALLS
ARE MADE BY MALES.

MORE THAN
75%
OF ALL COUNTRIES ARE
NORTH OF THE EQUATOR.

ODDS OF BECOMING AN ASTRONAUT.
1 IN 12,000,000

THE AVERAGE AMERICAN KID CATCHES 6 COLDS A YEAR; THE AVERAGE KID IN DAYCARE CATCHES
10.

ODDS THAT A CELEBRITY
MARRIAGE WILL
LAST A LIFETIME.

1 IN 3

- - - - - - - - - - - - - - - - - -

CATS HAVE OVER

100

VOCAL CHORDS.

THE CHANCE THAT A PUBLIC ROAD IS UNPAVED IN THE U.S. IS 1%, WHERE IT IS

75%

IN CANADA.

- - - - - - - - - - - - - - - - - - - -

THERE ARE

31,557,600

SECONDS IN A YEAR.

- - - - - - - - - - - - - - - - - - - -

ODDS AN ADULT BRUSHES THEIR TEETH AT WORK.

1 IN 7

35%
OF PEOPLE WATCHING TELEVISION YELL AT IT.

ODDS OF HAVING IDENTICAL QUADRUPLETS.
1 IN 15,000,000

ABOUT
70%
OF AMERICANS WHO GO TO COLLEGE DO IT TO MAKE MORE MONEY.

60%

OF AMERICAN BABIES ARE NAMED AFTER RELATIVES.

- -

8%

OF PEOPLE HAVE AN EXTRA RIB.

- -

AN AVERAGE CLOUD WEIGHS ABOUT

1,100,000

POUNDS, ROUGHLY EQUAL TO 100 ELEPHANTS.

1 OUT OF 8
LETTERS WRITTEN IS AN E.

- -

ODDS AN ADULT
HAS NO RELIGION.
1 IN 12

- -

THE AVERAGE SLEEPER
ROLLS OVER
12 TIMES
IN BED PER NIGHT.

80%

OF DEATHS IN U.S. CASINOS ARE CAUSED BY SUDDEN HEART ATTACKS.

44%

OF PEOPLE HAVE BROKEN A BONE.

0.3%

OF SOLAR ENERGY FROM THE SAHARA IS ENOUGH TO POWER ALL OF EUROPE.

ODDS OF BEING INJURED FROM MOWING THE LAWN.
1 IN 3,623

AVERAGE NUMBER OF CHILDREN CONCEIVED ON VALENTINE'S DAY.
11,000

SOUND TRAVELS
4.3 TIMES
FASTER THROUGH WATER THAN IN AIR.

46%

OF VIOLENCE ON TELEVISION OCCURS IN CARTOONS.

- -

ODDS AN ADULT SAYS THAT THEY
WOULD LIKE TO SPEND MORE
TIME DOING HOUSEWORK.

1 IN 50

3%
OF ALL PHOTOS TAKEN IN THE U.S. ARE TAKEN AT DISNEYLAND OR DISNEY WORLD.

- -

ODDS AN ADULT DOES NOT BELIEVE IN GHOSTS.

1 IN 1.5

- -

40%
OF AMSTERDAM COMMUTERS GET TO WORK BY BICYCLE.

58%
OF SCHOOL KIDS SAY PIZZA IS THEIR FAVORITE CAFETERIA FOOD.

- -

SIBERIA CONTAINS MORE THAN
25%
OF THE WORLD'S FORESTS.

85%

OF PHONE CALLS ARE CONDUCTED IN THE ENGLISH LANGUAGE.

55%

OF ALL MOVIES ARE RATED R.

ODDS AN ADULT PURCHASES ORGANIC FOOD ALL THE TIME.

1 IN 100

ON AVERAGE, A PERSON WOULD FILL TWO SWIMMING POOLS WITH 25,000 QUARTS OF SALIVA DURING THEIR LIFETIME.

- -

ODDS OF DATING A MILLIONAIRE.

1 IN 215

75%
OF AMERICAN HOUSEHOLDS
THE WOMEN MANAGE THE
MONEY AND PAY THE BILLS.

IT TAKES
492 SECONDS
FOR SUNLIGHT TO REACH THE EARTH.

ODDS OF FINDING A
PEARL IN AN OYSTER.
1 IN 12,000

59%

OF PEOPLE SAY THAT
THEY'RE AVERAGE LOOKING.

- -

ODDS OF WINNING $1
MILLION IN THE MCDONALD'S
MONOPOLY GAME.

1 IN 451,822,158

- -

THE RICHEST

1%

IN THE WORLD HAVE MORE WEALTH
THAN THE REST OF THE PLANET.

ODDS A FEMALE 20 OR YOUNGER GETS A MANICURE OR PEDICURE.

1 IN 12

63%

OF AMERICAN ADULTS WILL RENT AT LEAST 1 VIDEO THIS MONTH.

A BANANA CONTAINS

75%

WATER.

ODDS OF CATCHING A BALL AT A MAJOR LEAGUE BASEBALL GAME.

1 IN 563

COFFEE REPRESENTS

75%

OF ALL THE CAFFEINE CONSUMED IN THE U.S.

ODDS AN ADULT WILL
VISIT THE ER DUE TO A
POGO SITCK INJURY.
1 IN 115,300

- -

THE AVERAGE
HUMAN DRINKS OVER

16,000

GALLONS OF WATER
IN A LIFETIME.

THE AVERAGE AMERICAN
DOG WILL COST ITS OWNER
$14,600
IN ITS LIFETIME.

ODDS OF GETTING
A HOLE-IN-ONE.
1 IN 5,000

THERE ARE SOME
ICE CREAMS THAT ARE
75%
AIR.

25%

OF THE FISH YOU EAT ARE RAISED ON FISH FARMS.

- -

YOU USE

72

DIFFERENT MUSCLES WHILE SPEAKING.

ODDS OF FALLING
TO YOUR DEATH.
1 IN 119

- -

RICE IS THE
STAPLE FOOD FOR
50%
OF THE WORLD'S
POPULATION.

- -

ONE HUMAN HAIR
CAN SUPPORT
3 OUNCES.

THERE ARE
70,000,000
SHEEP IN NEW ZEALAND AND 4,000,000 PEOPLE.

ODDS THAT YOU WILL LIVE UNTIL YOU'RE 116.
1 IN 2,000,000,000

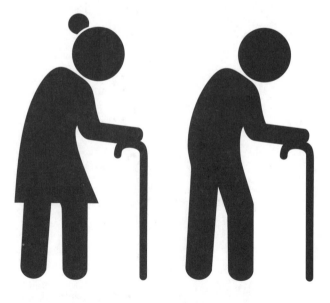

IN 1948,
2.3%
OF AMERICAN HOUSEHOLDS HAD TELEVISIONS.
TODAY 99% DO.

- -

ODDS OF WINNING $50,000 PLAYING PLINKO ON *THE PRICE IS RIGHT.*
1 IN 59,049

25%

OF WOMEN DON'T WASH THEIR HANDS AFTER USING A PUBLIC TOILET.

- -

ABOUT

8,000

AMERICANS ARE INJURED BY MUSICAL INSTRUMENTS EACH YEAR.

ODDS OF HAVING YOUR IDENTITY STOLEN.
1 IN 200

45,000
THUNDERSTORMS AROUND THE WORLD OCCUR EVERY DAY.

ODDS OF BEING DEALT A ROYAL FLUSH IN A FIRST HAND OF POKER.
1 IN 649,740

ODDS OF GETTING A PERFECT 29 HAND IN CRIBBAGE.
1 IN 216,580

12%
OF U.S. BUSINESSMEN WEAR THEIR TIES SO TIGHT THAT THEY RESTRICT THE BLOOD FLOW TO THEIR BRAIN.

ODDS OF DYING FROM FOOD POISONING.
1 IN 3,000,000

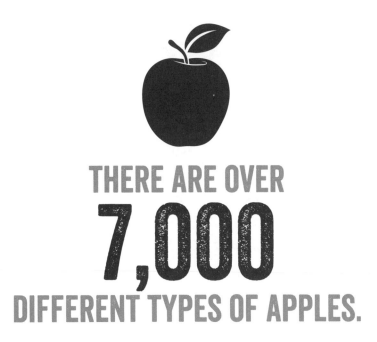

THERE ARE OVER
7,000
DIFFERENT TYPES OF APPLES.

- -

AMERICANS THROW AWAY
44,000,000
NEWSPAPERS A DAY.

- -

SUMMER ON
URANUS LASTS
21 YEARS.

1%
OF U.S. BUSINESSES ALLOW THEIR EMPLOYEES TO TAKE NAPS DURING WORKING HOURS.

- -

ITALY AND FRANCE PRODUCE OVER
40%
OF ALL WINE.

- -

THE AVERAGE AMERICAN EATS
263
EGGS A YEAR.

ODDS OF BEING INJURED FROM SHAVING.

1 IN 6,585

- -

ABOUT

39,000

GALLONS OF WATER ARE USED TO PRODUCE THE AVERAGE CAR.

ODDS OF GETTING ATTACKED BY A SHARK.
1 IN 3,748,067

THE IRS PROCESSES MORE THAN
2,000,000,000
PIECES OF PAPER EACH YEAR.

ODDS OF WINNING AN OLYMPIC GOLD MEDAL.
1 IN 662,000

- -

5%
OF AMERICANS SAY THEY "NEVER" MAKE THEIR BEDS.

- -

99%
OF INDIA'S TRUCK DRIVERS CAN'T READ ROAD SIGNS.

NEWBORN BABIES HAVE
350 BONES
AND BY THE AGE OF 5 HAVE MERGED TO 206.

ODDS OF DYING IN AN AIRPLANE CRASH.
1 IN 205,552

ODDS OF SHUFFLING A DECK OF CARDS INTO SEQUENTIAL ORDER.
1 IN 10^68

ONLY
30%
OF U.S. ADULTS ACTUALLY HAVE DANDRUFF WHILE 50% ARE "SELF-CONSCIOUS ABOUT IT."

- -

THE PENTAGON USES AN AVERAGE OF
666 ROLLS
OF TOILET PAPER EACH DAY.

ODDS OF AN ADULT BASEBALL FAN CHEERING FOR THE YANKEES.

1 IN 9.7

- -

ONLY 4 OUT OF

20,000

SPECIES OF BEES PRODUCE HONEY.

THE AVERAGE
AMERICAN MALE LAUGHS
69 TIMES
A DAY.

- -

ON AVERAGE,
THERE ARE
8 PEAS
IN A POD.

- -

33%
OF AMERICANS FLUSH THE
TOILET WHILE THEY'RE
STILL SITTING ON IT.

ODDS A WOMAN USES SEX TO GET HER MAN TO HELP WITH THE HOUSEWORK.

1 IN 1.2

- -

ODDS OF BEING KILLED BY A VENDING MACHINE.

1 IN 112,000,000

- -

52%

OF AMERICANS DRINK COFFEE.

ODDS OF BECOMING A U.S. PRESIDENT.

1 IN 10,000,000

AVERAGE NUMBER OF CHILDREN CONCEIVED ON VALENTINE'S DAY.

11,000

IF YOU PUT 23
PEOPLE IN A ROOM
THERE IS A

50%

CHANCE TWO WILL
SHARE A BIRTHDAY.

- -

ODDS OF BEING
MADE A SAINT.
1 IN 9,200,000

ODDS OF GETTING KILLED BY A COW.
1 IN 2,500,00

A FULL MOON IS
9 TIMES
BRIGHTER THAN A HALF MOON.

32%
OF WOMEN AND 8% OF MEN SAY THEY ARE BETTER AT DOING LAUNDRY THAN THEIR SPOUSE.

70%
OF BIRTHMARKS GRADUALLY FADE AWAY.

- -

THE ANNUAL GROWTH OF WWW TRAFFIC IS
314,000%.

- -

ODDS A MAN BELIEVES REAL MEN DON'T CRY.
1 IN 20

NIAGARA FALLS
COULD FILL

4,000

BATHTUBS
EVERY SECOND.

- -

2 OUT OF 5

PEOPLE MARRY
THEIR FIRST LOVE.

ODDS OF BECOMING A MOVIE STAR.
1 IN 1,505,000

- -

20%
OF MEN SAY THAT THEIR TV HAS TAUGHT THEM MORE ABOUT LIFE THAN THEIR PARENTS HAVE.

SEA WATER IS
APPROXIMATELY
3.5%
SALT.

ODDS OF DYING
FROM A BEE STING.
1 IN 6,100,000

ODDS AN ADULT WILL DRINK
AT LEAST ONE CUP OF
COFFEE DURING THE DAY.
1 IN 1.8

PEOPLE AGED

24-35

WORRY LESS THAN
ADULTS OF OTHER
AGE GROUPS.

- - - - - - - - - - - - - - - - - -

ODDS A PERSON HAS A
UNIQUE LAST NAME.

1 IN 67

- - - - - - - - - - - - - - - - - -

85%

OF PARENTS USE
CHILD SAFETY SEATS
INCORRECTLY.

THE AVERAGE AMERICAN FEMALE LAUGHS **55 TIMES** A DAY.

CUCUMBERS ARE **96%** WATER.

10% OF PEOPLE HAVE THROWN OUT A DISH JUST BECAUSE THEY DIDN'T FEEL LIKE WASHING IT.

ODDS THAT A FIRST MARRIAGE WILL SURVIVE WITHOUT SEPARATION OR DIVORCE FOR 15 YEARS.

1 IN 1.3

- -

ODDS AN ADULT CONSIDERS TRACK AND FIELD TO BE THEIR FAVORITE SPORT.

1 IN 100

THERE ARE
293
WAYS TO MAKE
CHANGE FOR A DOLLAR.

- - - - - - - - - - - - - - - - - - - -

IN 1900 THE
AVERAGE LIFE SPAN
IN THE U.S. WAS
47.

- - - - - - - - - - - - - - - - - - - -

ODDS A MAN HAS USED
A OUIJA BOARD TO
CONTACT THE DEAD.
1 IN 25

EVERY DAY
7%
OF THE U.S. POPULATION
EATS AT MCDONALDS.

- - - - - - - - - - - - - - - - - -

30%
OF PEOPLE REFUSE TO
SIT ON PUBLIC TOILET SEATS.

- - - - - - - - - - - - - - - - - -

ODDS OF DYING IN A
MOUNTAIN LION ATTACK
IN CALIFORNIA.
1 IN 32,000,000

THE EARTH IS STRUCK
BY LIGHTNING OVER
100 TIMES
EVERY SECOND.

- -

THE AVERAGE PERSON
MOVES THEIR RESIDENCE
11 TIMES IN THEIR LIFE,
ABOUT ONCE EVERY
6 YEARS.

1 IN 12
AMERICANS ALPHABETIZE THEIR SPICE RACK.

- -

THE U.S. SHREDS
7,000
TONS OF WORN-OUT CURRENCY EACH YEAR.

- -

CHOCOLATE MANUFACTURERS USE
40%
OF THE WORLDS ALMONDS.

ODDS AN ADULT HAS ELEVEN SIBLINGS.

1 IN 100

52%

OF PEOPLE HAVE MONEY INVESTED IN THE STOCK MARKET.

ODDS OF DYING BY A
FLESH-EATING BACTERIA.
1 IN 1,000,000

- -

ODDS OF INJURING YOURSELF
WITH A CHAINSAW.
1 IN 4,464

- -

THE AVERAGE PERSON HAS
10,000
TASTE BUDS.

ODDS A FEMALE IS 6'
3" TALL OR TALLER.

1 IN 1,101

32%

OF ALL LAND IN THE
U.S. IS OWNED BY
THE GOVERNMENT.

OVER

100

PEOPLE CHOKE TO DEATH ON
BALLPOINT PENS EACH YEAR.

ODDS OF BEING INJURED BY A TOLIET.
1 IN 10,000

THE LARGEST DIAMOND EVER FOUND WAS
3,106
CARATS.

IN 1950, ONLY 7% OF AMERICANS DYED THEIR HAIR, NOW **75%** DO.

ODDS THAT A LEFT-HANDED PERSON WILL DIE USING A RIGHT-HANDED APPLIANCE. **1 IN 4,400,000**

10% OF THE WORLD'S FOOD SUPPLY IS CONSUMED BY INSECTS.

ODDS A MILLENNIAL USES
THEIR CELL PHONE AT
A FAMILY DINNER.
1 IN 3.2

THE SHELL IS
12%
OF AN EGGS WEIGHT.

ODDS OF BEING CALLED
TO "COME ON DOWN!"
ON *THE PRICE IS RIGHT*.
1 IN 12

ODDS OF BEING
BORN WITH 11
FINGERS OR TOES.

1 IN 500

- -

80%
OF ALL PEOPLE HIT
BY LIGHTNING
ARE MEN.

50%
OF ALL FOREST FIRES ARE STARTED BY LIGHTNING.

- -

THE AVERAGE PERSON GOES TO THE TOILET
6 TIMES
PER DAY.

- -

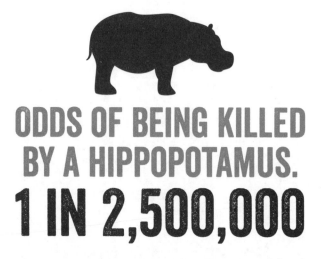

ODDS OF BEING KILLED BY A HIPPOPOTAMUS.
1 IN 2,500,000

THE AVERAGE AMERICAN'S DIET CONSISTS OF
55%
JUNK FOOD.

90%
OF THE WORLD'S POPULATION KISSES.

ODDS A MALE IS 6' 6" TALL OR TALLER.
1 IN 513

57%
OF WOMEN WOULD RATHER
GO ON A SHOPPING
SPREE THAN HAVE SEX.

- -

YOU SHED A COMPLETE
LAYER OF SKIN EVERY
4 WEEKS.

- -

EACH YEAR, MORE THAN
50,000
PEOPLE ARE INJURED BY
JEWELRY IN THE U.S.

25%
OF AMERICAN MEN ARE NOW SIX FEET OR TALLER COMPARED TO ONLY 4% IN 1900.

70%
OF PEOPLE CONSIDER THEMSELVES DOG PEOPLE.

IN AN AVERAGE HOUR,
THERE ARE OVER

61,000

AMERICANS AIRBORNE
OVER THE U.S.

- - - - - - - - - - - - - - - - - - - -

5%

OF AMERICANS NEVER
GET MARRIED.

- - - - - - - - - - - - - - - - - - - -

GOOGLE HAS OVER

2,000,000,000,000

SEARCHES PER YEAR.

48%
OF MEN THINK BALDING HAS A NEGATIVE EFFECT ON BUSINESS AND SOCIAL RELATIONSHIPS.

- -

ODDS AN ADULT BELIEVED IN SANTA CLAUS AS A CHILD.

1 IN 2

THE OPPOSITE SIDES OF A
DIE ALWAYS ADDS UP TO
7.

TOILETS USE
35%
OF INDOOR WATER USE.

2.6%
OF WALMART APPLICANTS
ARE ACCEPTED.

24%

OF COMMUTERS SAY THAT WHEN STUCK IN TRAFFIC, THEY THINK "DEEP THOUGHTS."

IT WOULD TAKE

1,200,000

MOSQUITOES, EACH SUCKING AT ONCE, TO COMPLETELY DRAIN THE BLOOD IN AN AVERAGE HUMAN.

45%
OF PEOPLE USE MOUTHWASH DAILY.

- -

ODDS A CHILD UNDER THE AGE OF 15 WILL VISIT THE E.R. DUE TO A TABLE IN A YEAR.

1 IN 366

- -

53%
OF AMERICANS THINK THEY ARE PAID THE RIGHT AMOUNT.

ODDS OF BEING KILLED BY A FALLING COCONUT.
1 IN 50,700,000

- -

THE AVERAGE PERSON SWALLOWS
295
TIMES DURING A MEAL.

- -

A SNAIL CAN SLEEP FOR
3 YEARS.

ODDS A TEENAGE BOY HAS NEVER BEEN KISSED.

1 IN 2.9

- -

NEARLY

6%

OF ALL MARRIAGE PROPOSALS ARE MADE OVER THE TELEPHONE.

GORILLAS SLEEP
14 HOURS
A DAY.

- -

29%
OF CALIFORNIA'S
AIR POLLUTION IS
FROM CHINA.

- -

ODDS THAT THE PRESIDENT
OF THE UNITED STATES
ATTENDED HARVARD.
1 IN 3.5

ODDS OF BEING CONSIDERED POSSESSED BY SATAN.
1 IN 7,000

ODDS A COLLEGE-BOUND SENIOR WHO TOOK THE ACT RECIEVED THE TOP SCORE.
1 IN 2,320

AMERICAN'S EAT
18,000,000,000
HOT DOGS A YEAR.

20%
OF CHINA'S PLANTS ARE USED IN MEDICINE.

- -

11%
OF PEOPLE ARE LEFT-HANDED.

THE LIFE SPAN OF A HOUSE FLY IS BETWEEN 10 TO 25 DAYS.

- - - - - - - - - - - - - - - - - -

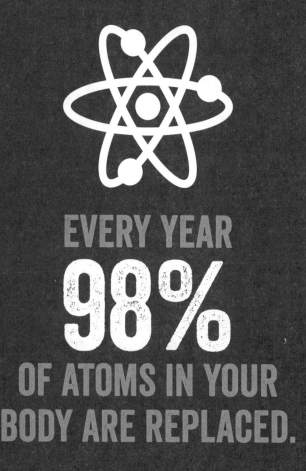

EVERY YEAR 98% OF ATOMS IN YOUR BODY ARE REPLACED.

CARROTS CONTAIN
0%
FAT.

- -

85%
OF PLANT
LIFE IS FOUND
IN THE OCEAN.

- -

ODDS AN ADULT VISITED A
PSYCHIATRIST IN THE PAST YEAR.
1 IN 22

EVERY YEAR
THE SUN LOSES
360,000,000
TONS OF MASS.

- -

IT TAKES
17 MUSCLES
TO SMILE AND
43 MUSCLES
TO FROWN.

ODDS OF FATALLY SLIPPING IN THE BATH OR SHOWER.
1 IN 2,232

- -

90%
OF ALL VOLCANIC ACTIVITY OCCURS IN THE OCEAN.

- -

THE AVERAGE PERSON IS A
28-YEAR-OLD
CHINESE MAN.